First World War
and Army of Occupation
War Diary
France, Belgium and Germany

33 DIVISION
Divisional Troops
Divisional Cyclist Company
27 July 1915 - 27 April 1916

WO95/2413/2

The Naval & Military Press Ltd
www.nmarchive.com
Published in association with The National Archives

Published by

The Naval & Military Press Ltd

Unit 10 Ridgewood Industrial Park,

Uckfield, East Sussex,

TN22 5QE England

Tel: +44 (0) 1825 749494

www.naval-military-press.com

www.nmarchive.com

This diary has been reprinted in facsimile from the original. Any imperfections are inevitably reproduced and the quality may fall short of modern type and cartographic standards.

© Crown Copyright

Images reproduced by permission of The National Archives, London, England, 2015.

Contents

Document type	Place/Title	Date From	Date To
Heading	WO95/2413/2		
Heading	33rd Division Divl Troops 33rd Divl Cyclist Coy Nov 1915-Apr 1916		
Heading	33rd Cyclist Vol 4		
Heading	33rd Divl Cyclist Vol I From July To Nov 15		
War Diary	Mansfield Notts	27/07/1915	27/07/1915
War Diary	Bulford	15/11/1915	15/11/1915
War Diary	Harve	16/11/1915	18/11/1915
War Diary	Steenbecque	19/11/1915	19/11/1915
War Diary	Morbecque	23/11/1915	23/11/1915
War Diary	Guarbecque	29/11/1915	30/11/1915
Heading	33rd Divl. Cyclist Vol 2		
War Diary	Bethune	02/12/1915	12/12/1915
War Diary	Cantrainne	12/12/1915	30/12/1915
War Diary	Bethune	31/12/1915	31/12/1915
Heading	33rd Cyclist Vol 3		
War Diary	Bethune	01/01/1916	28/02/1916
Heading	33 Div Cyclist Vol 5		
War Diary	Bethune	01/03/1916	30/04/1916
War Diary	Hesdin L'Abbe	27/04/1916	27/04/1916

Mop/9413(2)

Mop/9413(2)

33RD DIVISION
DIVL TROOPS

33RD DIVL CYCLIST COY.
NOV 1915 – APR 1916

33r Gebb
tot: 4

33rd Divl. Cyclists
vol I

121/7624

From July to Nov. 15.

WAR DIARY of 33rd Divisional Cyclist Company
~~INTELLIGENCE SUMMARY.~~

(Erase heading not required.)

From 27.7.15 to 1st December 15

Army Form C. 2118.

Instructions regarding War Diaries and Intelligence Summaries are contained in F.S. Regs., Part II. and the Staff Manual respectively. Title pages will be prepared in manuscript.

Volume 1.

Hour, Date, Place	Summary of Events and Information	Remarks and references to Appendices
27.7.1915 MANSFIELD. NOTTS	Company formed by transfer of Officers, N.C.O's and men from Infantry Battalions of the 33rd Division.	
11.15 AM 15.11.15 BULFORD	Entrained for SOUTHAMPTON	
3 AM 16.11.15 HARVE	Quartered No 5 Rest Camp.	
1.30 P.M. 18.11.15 HARVE	Entrained at GARE MARITIME	
11 AM 19.11.15 STEENBECQUE	Detrained and billeted at MORBECQUE	Ref: Map 36A 1/40000 FRANCE D 21 d 5.5.
23.11.15 MORBECQUE	Moved via STEENBECQUE – ST VENANT to HAMEAU DU PETIT CARLUY. GUARBECQUE	Ref: Map 36A 1/40000 FRANCE O 30 c 4.6.
29.11.15 GUARBECQUE	One Corporal, one Lance Corporal and twelve men attached to Headquarters Divisional Signal Company for dispatch riding	
30.11.15 GUARBECQUE	Moved from GUARBECQUE to BETHUNE. Headquarters at 77 Boulevard Victor Hugo.	

A. Pearce Gould CAPT.,
C.O. 33rd DIVISIONAL CYCLIST COY.

33rd Div L: Cyclists
Vol: 2

121
7910

WAR DIARY of the 33rd Divisional Cyclist Company Army Form C. 2118.
or
~~INTELLIGENCE SUMMARY.~~

(Erase heading not required.)

From 1st December to 1st January

Instructions regarding War Diaries and Intelligence Summaries are contained in F.S. Regs., Part II. and the Staff Manual respectively. Title pages will be prepared in manuscript.

Hour, Date, Place	Summary of Events and Information	Remarks and references to Appendices
2/12/15 BETHUNE	One Platoon detailed for Police Duties	
4/12/15 BETHUNE	Reconnoitered to line junction of RUE DU BOIS and RUE L'EPINETTE and PONT FIXE including both sides of LA BASSE Canal reporting what traffic roads will take and all new roads and those not shown on the map.	
9/12/15 BETHUNE	Received the following message:- "The Major General commanding has seen the road report sent in by you on the 6th and he considers it a very useful report." Collakin Major G.S.	I.G. 28 9.12.15
8/12/15 BETHUNE	One Officer and twenty men detailed for salvage work at LA QUINQUE RUE. Large quantity salved under Artillery fire.	MAP combined sheet BETHUNE 36 A SE 36 B NE V7 b 55
12/12/15 BETHUNE	Moved to CANTRAINNE headquarters at GUINBEZ HENRI. CANTRAINNE	
12/12/15 CANTRAINNE	Three Officers and five N.C.Os attended course of instruction Divisional Mounted Troops at BUSNES.	
19/12/15 Do	One N.C.O and six men detailed for bombing course.	
30/12/15 Do	Moved to BETHUNE billeted at FEUILLARD BARRACKS	
31/12/15 BETHUNE	Salvage Company formed and attached Cyclist Company for rations	

R. Pearce Serrold Capt.
O.C. 33rd Divisional Cyclist Coy.

33rd Cycho
vol 3

WAR DIARY
or
INTELLIGENCE SUMMARY.
(Erase heading not required.)

Army Form C. 2118.

33rd Divisional Cyclist Company

Hour, Date, Place	Summary of Events and Information	Remarks and references to Appendices
BETHUNE Jan'y 1st 1916	One N.C.O and 12 men as daily working party loading trail cars at 1st Corps Yard OUTREBONS	
2nd	One N.C.O and 12 men detailed as daily working party for C.R.E	
3rd	2nd Lieut J.K. Avery detailed as Officer i/c Divisional Trench Railways. One N.C.O and 8 men detailed for duty with O.C. Divisional Train for Charcoal Burning.	
4th	One N.C.O and 6 men detailed for Bombing Course at 98th Brigade Grenade School.	
5th	O.C. Company appointed Commandant FEUILLADE BARRACKS BETHUNE	
7th	One N.C.O and 10 men detailed for daily work at MARCOURT'S YARD. BETHUNE for making trench boards.	
16th	One N.C.O and 6 men detailed for Bombing Course at 98th Brigade Grenade School.	

WAR DIARY
or
INTELLIGENCE SUMMARY.
(Erase heading not required.)

Army Form C. 2118.

Instructions regarding War Diaries and Intelligence Summaries are contained in F.S. Regs., Part II. and the Staff Manual respectively. Title pages will be prepared in manuscript.

33 Divisional Cyclist Company

Hour, Date, Place	Summary of Events and Information	Remarks and references to Appendices
BETHUNE Jan 18th 1916	One N.C.O and 3 men to form guard to Coal Depot at BETHUNE	
Jany 20 – 22	No 1 Platoon under 2nd Lt H.W. West attached 18th Bn Royal Fusiliers 19th Infantry Brigade holding line between BRICKSTACKS and LA BASSÉE ROAD. Casualties Nil.	
Jany 20 – 22	No 2. Platoon under 2nd Lt L.D. Ollis attached 19th Bn Royal Fusiliers 98th Infantry Brigade, holding line from HUD TRENCH exclusive to BOYAU 9 inclusive on the left. Casualties Nil	
Jany 23 – 25	No 4 Platoon under Lt B.H. King attached 2nd Royal Welch Fusiliers 19th Infantry Brigade holding BRICKSTACKS. Casualties Nil	
Jany 26 – 28	No 3 Platoon 2nd Lt L.S. Brooke attached 1st Cameronians 19th Infantry Brigade, holding line left of BRICKSTACKS to RAILWAY. Casualties Nil	
Jany 26th	Orders received to "Stand by"	
Jany 29th	Above order cancelled.	

WAR DIARY
or
INTELLIGENCE SUMMARY.

(Erase heading not required.)

Army Form C. 2118.

Instructions regarding War Diaries and Intelligence Summaries are contained in F.S. Regs., Part II. and the Staff Manual respectively. Title pages will be prepared in manuscript.

33rd Divisional Cyclist Company.

Hour, Date, Place	Summary of Events and Information	Remarks and references to Appendices
BETHUNE Jan 27th 1916	One N.C.O and 15 men detailed to work under Divisional Signal Company as fatigue party	
Jany 31st – Feb 2.	No 6 Platoon under 2nd Lieut C.H. Watkins attached 16th Middlesex 100th Infantry Brigade holding line RAILWAY ALLEY to QUARRY Casualties One killed.	

[signed] CAPT.,
O.C. 33rd DIVISIONAL CYCLIST COY.

WAR DIARY of the 33rd Divisional Cyclist Coy Army Form C. 2118.
or
INTELLIGENCE SUMMARY.
(Erase heading not required.)

from 1st February to 1st March.

Hour, Date, Place	Summary of Events and Information	Remarks and references to Appendices
BÉTHUNE		
February 5th 1916	One N.C.O. and 6 men detailed for Instructional Course at 98th Bde Grenade School, BEUVRY	
February 10th 1916	One man detailed for clerical duty Divisional HdQrs "G" Office.	
February 11th 1916	One N.C.O. and 14 men for daily duty to C.R.E. BÉTHUNE.	
February 11th 1916	24 men trained as Guides to any reinforcements that may arrive in the Corps area during a battle.	G.S 13 — 33rd Div Hqrs. 11/2/16
February 12th 1916	One N.C.O and 15 men detailed for daily fatigue at Bomb Factory, BÉTHUNE	
February 12th 1916	4 N.C.O's detailed for Instructional Course at 98th Bde Machine Rifle School, BEUVRY	
February 19th – 25th	Working Party 2 Officers 60 N.C.Os and men detailed for duty with C.R.E. Trench repairs and construction.	
	Casualties. Nil	

WAR DIARY or INTELLIGENCE SUMMARY.

Army Form C. 2118.

Hour, Date, Place	Summary of Events and Information	Remarks and references to Appendices
BÉTHUNE February 20th 1916	4 N.C.O's and men detailed for Course at 98th Bde Lewis Machine Rifle School, BEUVRY.	
February 24th 1916	3 Men detailed for Divisional Signalling School, École de Jeunes Filles, BÉTHUNE.	
February 27th 1916	Draft: two men, reported from 3rd Infantry Base Depot	
February 27th 1916	Message AB900 received 1.5 P.M. "ADOPT THAW PRECAUTIONS" 15 Men detailed for control duties during thaw period 2.0 P.M February 27th to 6.0 A.M March 1st.	
February 28th 1916	4 N.C.O's and men detailed for Course at 98th Bde Lewis Machine Rifle School BEUVRY. No. of cases to date Invalided to England. FOUR men.	

Pearce Gould Capt.
O.C. 33rd DIVISIONAL CYCLIST COY.

33 DW
eyeless
vol 5

WAR DIARY or INTELLIGENCE SUMMARY.

(Erase heading not required.)

Army Form C. 2118.

33rd Divisional Cyclist Company.
March 1 to 31 — 1916.

Hour, Date, Place	Summary of Events and Information	Remarks and references to Appendices
March 1, 2, 3 and 4 BETHUNE	One Officer and 50 N.C.Os. and Men — working party attached Divisional Signals for Cable-laying to Trenches.	
7	30 N.C.Os. and Men —— do —— 1 Officer - Lewis Gun Course with 16th King's Royal Rifles. (ten days)	
8	1 Officer + 1 man - Lewis Gun Course - 98th Brigade School. (ten days)	
8 to 14	Supplied Guard (1 N.C.O. and 6 men) Divisional Bomb Store.	
9	1 N.C.O. and 15 men — Working Party attached to 222nd Field Coy. R.E.	
10 - 11	3 Officers, 1 Sergt. and 5 men — Surveying Reserve Line Trenches North of BEURRY — ANNEQUIN road.	
11 — 30	5 N.C.Os. and 25 men attached A.P.M. — Control and Examining Posts.	

(Continued)

WAR DIARY or INTELLIGENCE SUMMARY.

Army Form C. 2118.

33rd Divisional Cyclist Company
2.

Hour, Date, Place	Summary of Events and Information	Remarks and references to Appendices
March BETHUNE		
12	Two Officers to Divisional School of Instruction.	
15	One man to School of Cookery.	
16 – 17	One Officer, one Sergt. and four Men to Reserve Line Trenches South of BEUVRY – ANNEQUIN Road.	
17	1 Officer and 1 man – Lewis Gun Course – 98th Brigade.	
27 – 28	1 Officer + 50 N.C.Os + men – Working Party attached Divisional Signals. Trench Cables.	
31	——— do ——— Trench Cables.	
31	One man – School of Cookery.	
31	1 N.C.O. and 10 men attached A.P.M. – Control and Examining Posts.	
"	No. of Cases to date Invalided to ENGLAND – Five Men. Drafts taken on strength during March – 1 N.C.O. + 5 men. 1 N.C.O. sent ENGLAND for training at Cadet School.	

R.V. Edwards
CAPT.
For O.O. 33rd Divisional Cyclist Coy.

WAR DIARY or INTELLIGENCE SUMMARY

Army Form C. 2118.

33rd Divisional Cyclist Coy.

Hour, Date, Place	Summary of Events and Information	Remarks and references to Appendices
BETHUNE		
April 2	2nd Lieuts. J.S. BROOKE and J.R. AVERY for 15 days course at 33rd Divisional School of Instruction VENDIN-LEZ-BETHUNE.	
3	2nd Lieut. C.H. WATKINS takes over duties of Director of Trench Railways vice 2nd Lieut. J.R. AVERY.	
3.4.5	Working Parties 50 N.C.Os. and Men to trenches for Cable laying under direction of Divisional Signals.	
4	Three men of Cyclist Coy. placed under A.P.M. 33rd Division for traffic Control duties.	
5	One N.C.O. detailed to attend four days course at the Auto Gas School, AIRE.	
5	Draft from 3rd Infantry Base Depôt — Two men.	
5	One man detached as Orderly to Rev. B.G. O'Rorke Senior Chaplain, XI Corps.	
11	Working party — 30 N.C.Os. + men — for trench cabling under Divisional Signals.	
16.17.18	Working Parties — 50 N.C.Os. + men + 1 Officer — under 212th Coy. R.E.	

(Cont'd.)

WAR DIARY or INTELLIGENCE SUMMARY.

(Erase heading not required.)

Army Form C. 2118.

33rd Divisional Cyclist Coy.

2.

Hour, Date, Place	Summary of Events and Information	Remarks and references to Appendices
BETHUNE April 17	2nd Lieuts. J.S. BROOKE, J.R. AVERY and C.H. WATKINS returned to duty with the Company.	
(10 a.m.) 18	Advance Party under 2nd Lieut. H.W. WEST left FEUILLADE BARRACKS, BETHUNE for COYECQUES and HESDIN L'ABBÉ (Map 1/100,000 HAZEBROUCK 5A (CALAIS B)) Three days rations carried.	
(9.0 a.m.) 19	Company left FEUILLADE BARRACKS, BETHUNE and proceeded via LILLERS - ST HILAIRE - RELY - ESTRÉE-BLANCHE to COYECQUES reaching last place at 3.0 p.m. and billeting there for night. (Map 1/100,000 HAZEBROUCK 5A)	
(9.0 a.m.) 20	Company left COYECQUES and proceeded via FAUQUEMBERGUES - CAMPAGNE-LEZ-BOULONNAIS - ZOTEUX - SAMER to HESDIN L'ABBÉ (Map Calais 13 1/100,000), reaching last place at 5.0 p.m., and reporting to 1st Cavalry Division, Mounted Troops School.	
21 to 30	Course at School.	
25	Captain L.B. WEST (from 35th Div. Cyclist Coy) joins, but by order of Major NEWMAN, O.C. 33rd Divisional Mounted Troops, Capt. R.O. EDWARDS retains command.	

(Contd.)

WAR DIARY or INTELLIGENCE SUMMARY.

Army Form C. 2118.

55th Divisional Mounted Troops

Hour, Date, Place	Summary of Events and Information	Remarks and references to Appendices
HESDIN L'ABBÉ April 27	3 2nd Lieut. H.W. WEST to Intelligence Dept. G.H.Q. R.P. Edwards. Capt.	

www.ingramcontent.com/pod-product-compliance
Lightning Source LLC
Chambersburg PA
CBHW081252170426
4391CB00037B/2132